The Sunset Limited

CORMAC McCARTHY

The Sunset Limited

A NOVEL IN DRAMATIC FORM

PICADOR

First published 2006 by Vintage Books, a division of Random House, Inc., New York,
and simultaneously in Canada by Random House of Canada Limited, Toronto

First published in Great Britain 2010 by Picador
an imprint of Pan Macmillan, a division of Macmillan Publishers Limited
Pan Macmillan, 20 New Wharf Road, London N1 9RR
Basingstoke and Oxford
Associated companies throughout the world
www.macmillan.com

ISBN 978-0-330-51807-9

3 5 7 9 8 6 4 2

A CIP catalogue record for this book is available from
the British Library.

Printed in the UK by CPI Mackays, Chatham ME5 8TD

The Sunset Limited

This is a room in a tenement building in a black ghetto in New York City. There is a kitchen with a stove and a large refrigerator. A door to the outer hallway and another presumably to a bedroom. The hallway door is fitted with a bizarre collection of locks and bars. There is a cheap formica table in the room and two chrome and plastic chairs. There is a drawer in the table. On the table is a bible and a newspaper. A pair of glasses. A pad and pencil. A large black man is sitting in one chair (stage right) and in the other a middle-aged white man dressed in running pants and athletic shoes. He wears a T-shirt and the jacket—which matches the pants—hangs on the chair behind him.

Black   So what am I supposed to do with you, Professor?

White   Why are you supposed to do anything?

Black   I done told you. This aint none of my doin. I left out of here this mornin to go to work you wasnt no part of my plans at all. But here you is.

White   It doesnt mean anything. Everything that happens doesnt mean something else.

3

Black   Mm hm. It dont.

White   No. It doesnt.

Black   What's it mean then?

White   It doesnt mean anything. You run into people and maybe some of them are in trouble or whatever but it doesnt mean that you're responsible for them.

Black   Mm hm.

White   Anyway, people who are always looking out for perfect strangers are very often people who wont look out for the ones they're supposed to look out for. In my opinion. If you're just doing what you're supposed to then you dont get to be a hero.

Black   And that would be me.

White   I dont know. Would it?

Black   Well, I can see how they might be some truth in that. But in this particular case I might say I sure didnt know what sort of person I was supposed to be on the lookout for or what I was supposed to do when I found him. In this particular case they wasnt but one thing to go by.

White   And that was?

Black   That was that there he is standin there. And I can look at him and I can say: Well, he dont *look* like my brother. But there he is. Maybe I better look again.

White   And that's what you did.

Black   Well, you was kindly hard to ignore. I got to say that your approach was pretty direct.

White   I didnt approach you. I didnt even see you.

Black   Mm hm.

White   I should go. I'm beginning to get on your nerves.

Black   No you aint. Dont pay no attention to me. You seem like a sweet man, Professor. I reckon what I dont understand is how come you to get yourself in such a fix.

White   Yeah.

Black   Are you okay? Did you sleep last night?

White   No.

Black   When did you decide that today was the day? Was they somethin special about it?

White   No. Well. Today is my birthday. But I certainly dont regard that as special.

Black   Well happy birthday, Professor.

White   Thank you.

Black   So you seen your birthday was comin up and that seemed like the right day.

White   Who knows? Maybe birthdays are dangerous. Like Christmas. Ornaments hanging from the trees, wreaths from the doors, and bodies from the steampipes all over America.

Black   Mm. Dont say much for Christmas, does it?

White   Christmas is not what it used to be.

Black   I believe that to be a true statement. I surely do.

White   I've got to go.

He gets up and takes his jacket off the back of the chair and lifts it over his shoulders and then puts his arms in the sleeves rather than putting his arms in first one at a time.

Black   You always put your coat on like that?

White   What's wrong with the way I put my coat on?

Black   I didnt say they was nothin wrong with it. I just wondered if that was your regular method.

White   I dont have a regular method. I just put it on.

Black   Mm hm.

White   It's what, effeminate?

Black   Mm.

White   What?

Black   Nothin. I'm just settin here studyin the ways of professors.

White   Yeah. Well, I've got to go.

The black gets up.

Black   Well. Let me get my coat.

White   Your coat?

Black   Yeah.

White   Where are you going?

Black   Goin with you.

White   What do you mean? Going with me where?

Black   Goin with you wherever you goin.

White   No you're not.

Black   Yeah I am.

White   I'm going home.

Black   All right.

White   All right? You're not going home with me.

Black   Sure I am. Let me get my coat.

White   You cant go home with me.

Black   Why not?

White   You cant.

Black   What. You can go home with me but I cant go home with you?

White   No. I mean no, that's not it. I just need to go home.

Black   You live in a apartment?

White   Yes.

Black   What. They dont let *black* folks in there?

White   No. I mean of course they do. Look. No more jokes. I've got to go. I'm very tired.

Black   Well I just hope we dont run into no hassle about you gettin me in there.

White   You're serious.

Black   Oh I think you know I'm serious.

White   You cant be serious.

Black   I'm as serious as a heart attack.

White   Why are you doing this?

Black   Me? I aint got no choice in the matter.

White   Of course you have a choice.

Black   No I aint.

White   Who appointed you my guardian angel?

Black   Let me get my coat.

White Answer the question.

Black You *know* who appointed me. I didnt ask for you to leap into my arms down in the subway this mornin.

White I didnt leap into your arms.

Black You didnt?

White No. I didnt.

Black Well how did you get there then?

The professor stands with his head lowered. He looks at the chair and then turns and goes and sits down in it.

Black What. Now we aint goin?

White Do you really think that Jesus is in this room?

Black No. I dont think he's in this room.

White You dont?

Black I *know* he's in this room.

The professor folds his hands at the table and lowers his head. The black pulls out the other chair and sits again.

Black   Its the way you put it, Professor. Be like me askin you do you *think* you got your coat on. You see what I'm sayin?

White   It's not the same thing. It's a matter of agreement. If you and I say that I have my coat on and Cecil says that I'm naked and I have green skin and a tail then we might want to think about where we should put Cecil so that he wont hurt himself.

Black   Who's Cecil?

White   He's not anybody. He's just a hypothetical . . . There's not any Cecil. He's just a person I made up to illustrate a point.

Black   Made up.

White   Yes.

Black   Mm.

White   We're not going to get into this again are we? It's not the same thing. The fact that I made Cecil up.

Black   But you did make him up.

White   Yes.

Black   And his view of things dont count.

White   No. That's why I made him up. I could have changed it around. I could have made you the one that didnt think I was wearing a coat.

Black   And was green and all that shit you said.

White   Yes.

Black   But you didnt.

White   No.

Black   You loaded it off on Cecil.

White   Yes.

Black   But Cecil cant defend hisself cause the fact that he aint in agreement with everbody else makes his word no good. I mean aside from the fact that you made him up and he's green and everthing.

White   He's not the one who's green. I am. Where is this going?

Black   I'm just tryin to find out about Cecil.

White   I dont think so. Can you see Jesus?

Black   No. I cant see him.

White   But you talk to him.

Black   I dont miss a day.

White   And he talks to you.

Black   He has talked to me. Yes.

White   Do you hear him? Like out loud?

Black   Not out loud. I dont hear a voice. I dont hear my own, for that matter. But I have heard him.

White   Well why couldnt Jesus just be in your head?

Black   He is in my head.

White   Well I don't understand what it is that you're trying to tell me.

Black   I know you dont, honey. Look. The first thing you got to understand is that I aint got a original thought in my head. If it aint got the lingerin scent of divinity to it then I aint interested.

White   The lingering scent of divinity.

13

Black   Yeah. You like that?

White   It's not bad.

Black   I heard it on the radio. *Black* preacher. But the point is I done tried it the other way. And I dont mean chippied, neither. Runnin blindfold through the woods with the bit tween your teeth. Oh man. Didnt I try it though. If you can find a soul that give it a better shot than me I'd like to meet him. I surely would. And what do you reckon it got me?

White   I dont know. What did it get you?

Black   Death in life. That's what it got me.

White   Death in life.

Black   Yeah. Walkin around death. Too dead to even know enough to lay down.

White   I see.

Black   I dont think so. But let me ask you this question.

White   All right.

Black   Have you ever read this book?

White   I've read parts of it. I've read in it.

Black   Have you ever read it?

White   I read *The Book of Job*.

Black   Have. You. Ever. Read. It.

White   No.

Black   But you is read a lot of books.

White   Yes.

Black   How many would you say you read?

White   I've no idea.

Black   Ball park.

White   I dont know. Two a week maybe. A hundred a year. For close to forty years.

The black takes up his pencil and licks it and falls to squinting at his pad, adding numbers laboriously, his tongue in the corner of his mouth, one hand on his head.

White   Forty times a hundred is four thousand.

Black   (*Almost laughing*) I'm just messin with you, Professor. Give me a number. Any number you like. And I'll give you forty times it back.

White   Twenty-six.

Black   A thousand and forty.

White   A hundred and eighteen.

Black   Four thousand seven hundred and twenty.

White   Four thousand seven hundred and twenty.

Black   Yeah.

White   The answer is the question.

Black   Say what?

White   That's your new number.

Black   Four thousand seven hundred and twenty?

White   Yes.

Black   That's a big number, Professor.

White   Yes it is.

Black   Do you know the answer?

White   No. I dont.

Black   It's a hundred and eighty-eight thousand and eight hundred.

They sit.

White   Let me have that.

The black slides the pad and pencil across the table. The professor does the figures and looks at them and looks at the black. He slides the pencil and paper back across the table and sits back.

White   How do you do that?

Black   Numbers is the *black* man's friend. Butter and eggs. Crap table. You quick with numbers you can put the mojo on you brother. Confiscate the contents of his pocketbook. You get a lot of time to practice that shit in the jailhouse.

White   I see.

Black   But let's get back to all them books you done read. You think maybe you read four thousand books.

White   Probably. Maybe more than that.

Black   But you aint read this one.

White   No. Not the whole book. No.

Black   Why is that?

White   I dont know.

Black   What would you say is the best book that ever was wrote?

White   I have no idea.

Black   Take a shot.

White   There are a lot of good books.

Black   Well pick one.

White   Maybe *War and Peace.*

Black   All right. You think that's a better book than this one?

White   I dont know. They're different kinds of books.

Black   This *War and Peace* book. That's a book that somebody made up, right?

White   Well, yes.

Black   So is that how it's different from this book?

White   Not really. In my view they're both made up.

Black   Mm. Aint neither one of em true.

White   Not in the historical sense. No.

Black   So what would be a true book?

White   I suppose maybe a history book. Gibbon's *Decline and Fall of the Roman Empire* might be one. At least the events would be actual events. They would be things that had happened.

Black   Mm hm. You think that book is as good a book as this book here?

White   The bible.

Black   The bible.

White   I dont know. Gibbon is a cornerstone. It's a major book.

Black   And a true book. Dont forget that.

White   And a true book. Yes.

Black   But is it as good a book.

White   I dont know. I dont know as you can make a comparison. You're talking about apples and pears.

Black   No we aint talkin bout no apples and pears, Professor. We talkin bout books. Is that *Decline and Fall* book as good a book as this book here. Answer the question.

White   I might have to say no.

Black   It's more true but it aint as good.

White   If you like.

Black   It aint what I like. It's what you said.

White   All right.

The black lays the bible back down on the table.

Black   It used to say here on the cover fore it got wore off: The greatest book ever written. You think that might be true?

White   It might.

Black   You read good books.

White   I try to. Yes.

Black   But not the best book. Why is that?

White   I need to go.

Black   You dont need to go, Professor. Stay here and visit with me.

White   You're afraid I'll go back to the train station.

Black   You might. Just stay with me.

White   What if I promised I wouldnt?

Black   You might anyways.

White   Dont you have to go to work?

Black   I was on my way to work.

White   A funny thing happened to you on your way to work.

Black   Yes it did.

White   Will they fire you?

Black   Naw. They aint goin fire me.

White   You could call in.

Black   Aint got a phone. Anyways, they know if I aint there I aint comin. I aint a late sort of person.

White   Why dont you have a phone?

Black   I dont need one. The junkies'd steal it anyways.

White   You could get a cheap one.

Black   You cant get too cheap for a junky. But let's get back to you.

White   Let's stick with you for a minute.

Black   All right.

White   Can I ask you something?

Black   Sure you can.

White   Where were you standing? I never saw you.

Black   You mean when you took your amazin leap?

White   Yes.

Black   I was on the platform.

White   On the platform.

Black   Yeah.

White   Well I didnt see you.

Black   I was just standin there on the platform. Mindin my own business. And here you come. Haulin ass.

White   I'd looked all around to make sure there was no one there. Particularly no children. There was nobody around.

Black   Nope. Just me.

White   Well I dont know where you could have been.

Black   Mm. Professor you fixin to get spooky on me now. Maybe I was behind a post or somethin.

White   There wasnt any post.

Black   So what are we sayin here? You lookin at some big *black* angel got sent down here to grab your honky ass out of the air at the last possible minute and save you from destruction?

White   No. I dont think that.

Black   Such a thing aint possible.

White   No. It isnt.

Black   Well you the one suggested it.

White   I didnt suggest any such thing. You're the one put in the stuff about angels. I never said anything about angels. I dont believe in angels.

Black   What is it you believe in?

White   A lot of things.

Black   All right.

White   All right what?

Black   All right what things.

White   I believe in things.

Black   You said that.

White   Probably I dont believe in a lot of things that I used to believe in but that doesnt mean I dont believe in anything.

Black   Well give me a for instance.

White   Mostly the value of things.

Black   Value of things.

White   Yes.

Black   Okay. What things.

White   Lots of things. Cultural things, for instance. Books and music and art. Things like that.

Black   All right.

White   Those are the kinds of things that have value to me. They're the foundations of civilization. Or they used to have value. I suppose they dont have so much any more.

Black   What happened to em?

White   People stopped valuing them. I stopped valuing them. To a certain extent. I'm not sure I could tell you why. That world is largely gone. Soon it will be wholly gone.

Black   I aint sure I'm followin you, Professor.

White   There's nothing to follow. It's all right. The things that I loved were very frail. Very fragile. I didnt know that. I thought they were indestructible. They werent.

Black   And that's what sent you off the edge of the platform. It wasnt nothin personal.

White   It is personal. That's what an education does. It makes the world personal.

Black   Hm.

White   Hm what.

Black   Well. I was just thinkin that them is some pretty powerful words. I dont know that I got a answer about any of that and it might be that they aint no answer. But still I got to ask what is the use of notions such as them if it wont keep you glued down to the platform when the Sunset Limited comes through at eighty mile a hour.

White   Good question.

Black   I thought so.

White   I dont have an answer to any of that either. Maybe it's not logical. I dont know. I dont care. I've been asked didnt I think it odd that I should be present to witness the death of every-thing and I do think it's odd but that doesnt mean it's not so. Someone has to be here.

Black   But you dont intend to stick around for it.

White   No. I dont.

Black   So let me see if I got this straight. You sayin that all this culture stuff is all they ever was tween you and the Sunset Limited.

White   It's a lot.

Black   But it busted out on you.

White   Yes.

Black   You a culture junky.

White   If you like. Or I was. Maybe you're right. Maybe I have no beliefs. I believe in the Sunset Limited.

Black   Damn, Professor.

White   Damn indeed.

Black   No beliefs.

White   The things I believed in dont exist any more. It's foolish to pretend that they do. Western Civilization finally went up in smoke in the chimneys at Dachau but I was too infatuated to see it. I see it now.

Black   You a challenge, Professor. Did you know that?

White   Well, there's no reason for you to become involved in my problems. I should go.

Black   You got any friends?

White   No.

Black   You aint got even one friend?

White   No.

Black   You got to be kiddin me, Professor. Not one?

White   Not really. No.

Black   Well tell me about that one.

White   What one?

Black   The not really one.

White   I have a friend at the university. Not a close friend. We have lunch from time to time.

Black   But that's about as good as it gets.

White   What do you mean?

Black   That's about all you got in the way of friends.

White   Yes.

Black   Mm. Well. If that's the best friend you got then I reckon that's your best friend. Aint it?

White   I dont know.

Black   What did you do to him.

White   What did I do to him?

Black   Yeah.

White   I didnt do anything to him.

Black   Mm hm.

White   I didnt do anything to him. What makes you think I did something to him?

Black   I dont know. Did you?

White   No. What is it you think I did to him?

Black   I dont know. I'm waitin on you to tell me.

White   Well there's nothing to tell.

Black   But you didnt leave him no note or nothin. When you decided to take the train.

White   No.

Black   Your best friend?

White   He's not my best friend.

Black   I thought we just got done decidin that he was.

White   *You* just got done deciding.

Black   You ever tell him you was thinkin about this?

White   No.

Black   Damn, Professor.

White   Why should I?

Black   I dont know. Maybe cause he's your best friend?

White   I told you. We're not all that close.

Black   Not all that close.

White   No.

Black   He's your best friend only you aint all that close.

White   If you like.

Black   Not to where you'd want to bother him about a little thing like dyin.

White   *(Looking around the room)* Look. Suppose I were to give you my word that I would just go home and that I wouldnt try to kill myself en route.

Black   Suppose I was to give you my word that I wouldnt listen to none of your bullshit.

White   So what am I, a prisoner here?

Black   You know bettern that. Anyway, you was a prisoner fore you got here. Death Row prisoner. What did your daddy do?

White   What?

Black   I said what did your daddy do. What kind of work.

White   He was a lawyer.

Black   Lawyer.

White   Yes.

Black   What kind of law did he do?

White   He was a government lawyer. He didnt do criminal law or things like that.

Black   Mm hm. What would be a thing *like* criminal law?

White   I dont know. Divorce law, maybe.

Black   Yeah. Maybe you got a point. What did he die of?

White   Who said he was dead?

Black   Is he dead?

White   Yes.

Black   What did he die of?

White   Cancer.

Black   Cancer. So he was sick for a while.

White   Yes. He was.

Black   Did you go see him?

White   No.

Black   How come?

White   I didnt want to.

Black   Well how come you didnt want to?

White   I dont know. I just didnt. Maybe I didnt want to remember him that way.

Black   Bullshit. Did he ask you to come?

White   No.

Black   But your mama did.

White   She may have. I dont remember.

Black   Come on, Professor. She asked you to come.

White   Okay. Yes.

Black   And what did you tell her?

White   I told her I would.

Black   But you didnt.

White   No.

Black   How come?

White   He died.

Black   Yeah, but that aint it. You had time to go see him and you didnt do it.

White   I suppose.

Black   You waited till he was dead.

White   Okay. So I didnt go and see my father.

Black   Your daddy is layin on his deathbed dyin of cancer. Your mama settin there with him. Holdin his hand. He in all kinds of pain. And they ask you to come see him one last time fore he dies and you tell em no. You aint comin. Please tell me I got some part of this wrong.

White   If that's the way you want to put it.

Black   Well how would you put it?

White   I dont know.

Black   That's the way it is. Aint it?

White   I suppose.

Black   No you dont suppose. Is it or aint it?

White   Yes.

Black   Well. Let me see if I can find my train schedule.

He opens the table drawer and rummages through it.

Black   See when that next uptown express is due.

White   I'm not sure I see the humor.

Black   I'm glad to hear you say that, Professor. Cause I aint sure either. I just get more amazed by the minute, that's all. How come you cant *see* yourself, honey? You plain as glass. I can see the wheels turnin in there. The gears. And I can see the light too. Good light. True light. Cant you see it?

White   No. I cant.

Black   Well bless you, brother. Bless you and keep you. Cause it's there.

They sit.

White   When were you in the penitentiary?

Black   Long time ago.

White   What were you in for?

Black   Murder.

White   Really?

Black   Now who would claim to be a murderer that wasnt one?

White   You called it the jailhouse.

Black   Yeah?

White   Do most *black*s call the penitentiary the jailhouse?

Black   Naw. Just us old country niggers. We kind of make it a point to call things for what they is. I'd hate to guess how many names they is for the jailhouse. I'd hate to have to count em.

White   Do you have a lot of jailhouse stories?

Black   Jailhouse stories.

White   Yes.

Black   I dont know. I used to tell jailhouse stories some but they kindly lost their charm. Maybe we ought to talk about somethin more cheerful.

White   Have you ever been married?

Black   Married.

White   Yes.

Black   *(Softly)* Oh man.

White   What.

Black   Maybe we ought to take another look at them jailhouse stories. *(He shakes his head, laughing soundlessly. He pinches the bridge of his nose, his eyes shut.)* Oh my.

White   Do you have any children?

Black   Naw, Professor, I aint got nobody. Everbody in my family is dead. I had two boys. They been dead for years. Just about everbody I ever knowed is dead, far as that goes. You might want to think about that. I might be a hazard to your health.

White   You were always in a lot of trouble?

Black   Yeah. I was. I liked it. Maybe I still do. I done seven years hard time and I was lucky not to of done a lot more. I hurt a lot of people. I'd smack em around a little and then they wouldnt get up again.

37

White   But you dont get in trouble now.

Black   No.

White   But you still like it?

Black   Well, maybe I'm just condemned to it. Bit in the ass by my own karma. But I'm on the other side now. You want to help people that's in trouble you pretty much got to go where the trouble is at. You aint got a lot of choice.

White   And you want to help people in trouble.

Black   Yeah.

White   Why is that?

The black tilts his head and studies him.

Black   You aint ready for that.

White   How about just the short answer.

Black   That is the short answer.

White   How long have you been here?

Black   You mean in this buildin?

White   Yes.

Black   Six years. Seven, almost.

White   I dont understand why you live here.

Black   As compared to where?

White   Anywhere.

Black   Well I'd say this pretty much is anywhere. I could live in another buildin I reckon. This is all right. I got a bedroom where I can get away. Got a sofa yonder where people can crash. Junkies and crackheads, mostly. Of course they goin to carry off your portables so I dont own nothin. And that's good. You hang out with the right crowd and you'll finally get cured of just about ever cravin. They took the refrigerator one time but somebody caught em on the stairs with it and made em bring it back up. Now I got that big sucker yonder. Traded up. Only thing I miss is the music. I aim to get me a steel door for the bedroom. Then I can have me some music again. You got to get the door and the frame together. I'm workin on that. I dont care nothin about television but I miss that music.

White   You dont think this is a terrible place?

Black   Terrible?

White   Yes.

Black   What's terrible about it?

White   It's horrible. It's a horrible life.

Black   Horrible life?

White   Yes.

Black   Damn, Professor. This aint a horrible life. What you talkin bout?

White   This place. It's a horrible place. Full of horrible people.

Black   Oh my.

White   You must know these people are not worth saving. Even if they could be saved. Which they cant. You must know that.

Black   Well, I always liked a challenge. I started a ministry in prison fore I got out. Now that was a challenge. Lot of the brothers'd show up that they didnt really care nothin bout it. They couldnt of cared less bout the word of God. They just wanted it on their resumé.

White Resumé?

Black Resumé. You had brothers in there that had done some real bad shit and they wasnt sorry about a damn thing cept gettin caught. Of course the funny thing was a lot of em did believe in God. Maybe even more than these folks here on the outside. I know I did. You might want to think about that, Professor.

White I think I'd better go.

Black You dont need to go, Professor. What am I goin to do, you leave me settin here by myself?

White You dont need me. You just dont want to feel responsible if anything happens to me.

Black What's the difference?

White I dont know. I just need to go.

Black Just stay a while. This place is got to be more cheerful than you own.

White I dont think you have any idea how strange it is for me to be here.

Black   I think I got some idea.

White   I have to go.

Black   Let me ask you somethin.

White   All right.

Black   You ever had one of them days when things
          was just sort of weird all the way around?
          When things just kindly fell into place?

White   I'm not sure what you mean.

Black   Just one of them days. Just kind of magic. One
          of them days when everthing turns out right.

White   I dont know. Maybe. Why?

Black   I just wondered if maybe it aint been kindly a
          long dry spell for you. Until you finally took
          up with the notion that that's the way the
          world is.

White   The way the world is.

Black   Yeah.

White   And how is that?

Black   I dont know. Long and dry. The point is that even if it might seem that way to you you still got to understand that the sun dont shine up the same dog's ass ever day. You understand what I'm sayin?

White   If what you're saying is that I'm simply having a bad day that's ridiculous.

Black   I dont think you havin a bad day, Professor. I think you havin a bad life.

White   You think I should change my life.

Black   What, are you shittin me?

White   I have to go.

Black   You could hang with me here a little while longer.

White   What about my jailhouse story?

Black   You dont need to hear no jailhouse story.

White   Why not?

Black   Well, you kind of suspicious bout everthing. You think I'm fixin to put you in the trick bag.

White   And you're not.

43

Black   Oh no. I am. I just dont want you to know about it.

White   Well, in any case I need to go.

Black   You know you aint ready to hit the street.

White   I have to.

Black   I know you aint got nothin you got to do.

White   And how do you know that?

Black   Cause you aint even supposed to be here.

White   I see your point.

Black   What if I was to tell you a jailhouse story? You stay then?

White   All right. I'll stay for a while.

Black   My man. All right. Here's my jailhouse story.

White   Is it a true story?

Black   Oh yeah. It's a true story. I dont know no other kind.

White   All right.

Black   All right. I'm in the chowline and I'm gettin my chow and this nigger in the line behind me gets into it with the server. Says the beans is cold and he throws the ladle down in the beans. And when he done that they was beans splashed on me. Well, I wasnt goin to get into it over some beans but it did piss me off some. I'd just put on a clean suit—you know, khakis, shirt and trousers—and you only got two a week. And I did say somethin to him like hey man, watch it, or somethin like that. But I went on, and I'm thinkin, just let it go. Let it go. And then this dude says somethin to me and I turned and looked back at him and when I done that he stuck a knife in me. I never even seen it. And the blood is just flyin. And this aint no jailhouse shiv neither. It's one of them ital-ian switchblades. One of them *black* and silver jobs. And I didnt do a thing in the world but duck and step under the rail and I reached and got hold of the leg of this table and it come off in my hand just as easy. And it's got this big long screw stickin out of the end of it and I went to wailin on this nigger's head and I didnt quit. I beat on it till you couldnt hardly tell it was a head. And that screw'd stick in his head and I'd have to stand on him to pull it out again.

White   What did he say?

Black   What did he say?

White   I mean in the line. What did he say.

Black   I aint goin to repeat it.

White   That doesnt seem fair.

Black   Dont seem fair.

White   No.

Black   Hm. Well, here I'm tellin you a bonafide blood and guts tale from the Big House. The genuine article. And I cant get you to fill in the blanks about what this nigger said?

White   Do you have to use that word?

Black   Use that word.

White   Yes.

Black   We aint makin much progress here, is we?

White   It just seems unnecessary.

Black   You dont want to hear nigger but you about to bail out on me on account of I wont tell you some terrible shit the nigger said. You sure about this?

White   I just dont see why you have to say that word.

Black   Well it's my story aint it? Anyway I dont remember there bein no Afro-Americans or persons of color there. To the best of my recollection it was just a bunch of niggers.

White   Go ahead.

Black   Well at some point I had pulled the knife out and I reckon I'd done dropped it in the floor. I'm wailin on this nigger's head and all the time I'm doin that his buddy has got hold of me from behind. But I'm holdin on to the rail with one hand and I aint goin nowhere. Course what I dont know is that this other dude has picked up the knife and he's tryin to gut me with it. I finally felt the blood and I turned around and busted him in the head and he went skitterin off across the floor, and by now they done pushed the button and the alarm is goin and everbody's down on the floor and we're in lockdown and the guard up on the tier is got a shotgun pointed at me and he hollers at me to put down my weapon and get on the floor. And he's about to shoot me when the lieutenant comes in and hollers at him to hold his fire and he tells me to throw that club down and I looked around and I'm the only one standin. I seen the nigger's feet stickin out from under the servin counter where he'd

47

crawled so I throwed the thing down and I dont remember much after that. They told me I'd lost about half my blood. I remember slippin around in it but I thought it was this other dude's.

White   *(Dryly)* That's quite a story.

Black   Yeah. That's really just the introduction to the actual story.

White   Did the man die?

Black   No he didnt. Everbody lived. They thought he was dead but he wasnt. He never was right after that so I never had no more trouble out of him. He was missin a eye and he walked around with his head sort of sideways and one arm hangin down. Couldnt talk right. They finally shipped him off to another facility.

White   But that's not the whole story.

Black   No. It aint.

White   So what happened.

Black   I woke up in the infirmary. They had done operated on me. My spleen was cut open. Liver. I dont know what all. I come pretty close to dyin. And I had two hundred and eighty stitches holdin me together and I was hurtin. I didnt know you could hurt that bad. And still they got me in leg irons and got me handcuffed to the bed. If you can believe that. And I'm layin there and I hear this voice. Just as clear. Couldnt of been no clearer. And this voice says: If it was not for the grace of God you would not be here. Man. I tried to raise up and look around but of course I couldnt move. Wasnt no need to anyways. They wasnt nobody there. I mean, they was somebody there all right but they wasnt no use in me lookin around to see if I could see him.

White   You dont think this is a strange kind of story?

Black   I do think it's a strange kind of story.

White   What I mean is that you didnt feel sorry for this man?

Black   You gettin ahead of the story.

White   The story of how a fellow prisoner became a crippled one-eyed halfwit so that you could find God.

Black   Whoa.

49

White Well isnt it?

Black I dont know.

White You hadnt thought of it that way.

Black Oh I'd thought of it that way.

White And?

Black And what?

White Isnt that the real story?

Black Well. I dont want to get on the wrong side of you. You seem to have a powerful wish for that to be the real story. So I will say that that is certainly one way to look at it. I got to concede that. I got to keep you interested.

White String me along.

Black That okay with you?

White And then put me in the what was it? The trick bag?

Black Yeah.

White Right.

Black   You got to remember this is a jailhouse story.

White   All right.

Black   Which you specifically asked for.

White   All right.

Black   The point is, Professor, that I aint got the first notion in the world about what makes God tick. I dont know why he spoke to me. I wouldnt of.

White   But you listened.

Black   Well what choice would you have?

White   I dont know. Not listen?

Black   How you goin to do that?

White   Just dont listen.

Black   Do you think he goes around talkin to people that he knows aint goin to listen in the first place? You think he's got that kind of free time?

White   I see your point.

Black   If he didnt know I was ready to listen he wouldnt of said a word.

White   He's an opportunist.

Black   Meanin I guess that he seen somebody in a place low enough to where he ought to be ready to take a pretty big step.

White   Something like that.

Black   And you think that maybe I think that you might be in somethin like that kind of a place you own self.

White   Could be.

Black   Well I can dig that. I can dig it. Of course they is one small problem.

White   And that is.

Black   I aint God.

White   I'm glad to hear you say that.

Black   It come as a relief to me too.

White   Did you used to think you were God?

Black   No. I didnt. I didnt know what I was. But I thought I was in charge. I never knowed what that burden weighed till I put it down. That might of been the sweetest thing of all. To just hand over the keys.

White   Let me ask you something.

Black   Ask it.

White   Why cant you people just accept it that some people dont even *want* to believe in God.

Black   I accept that.

White   You do?

Black   Sure I do. Meanin that I believe it to be a fact. I'm lookin at it ever day. I better accept it.

White   Then why cant you leave us alone?

Black   To do your own thing.

White   Yes.

Black   Hangin from them steampipes and all.

White   If that's what we want to do, yes.

Black   Cause he said not to. It's in here. (*Holding up the book*)

The professor shakes his head.

Black   I guess you dont want to be happy.

White   Happy?

Black   Yeah. What's wrong with happy?

White   God help us.

Black   What. We done opened a can of worms here? What you got against bein happy?

White   It's contrary to the human condition.

Black.   Well. It's contrary to your condition. I got to agree with that.

White   Happy. This is ridiculous.

Black   Like they aint no such a thing.

White   No.

Black   Not for nobody.

White   No.

Black   Mm. How'd we get in such a fix as this?

White   We were born in such a fix as this. Suffering and human destiny are the same thing. Each is a description of the other.

Black   We aint talkin about sufferin. We talkin about bein happy.

White   Well you cant be happy if you're in pain.

Black   Why not?

White   You're not making any sense.

The black falls back clutching his chest.

Black   Oh them is some hard words from the professor. The preacher has fell back. He's clutchin his heart. Eyes is rolled back in his head. Wait a minute. Wait a minute folks. His eyes is blinkin. I think he's comin back. I think he's comin back.

The black sits up and leans forward.

Black   The point, Professor, is that if you didnt have no pain in your life then how would you even know you *was* happy? As compared to what?

White   You dont have anything to drink around here do you?

Black   No, Professor, I aint. You a drinkin man?

White   Are we about to get a temperance lecture?

Black   Not from me.

White   It's been a difficult day. I take it you dont drink.

Black   I dont. I have done my share of it in my time.

White   Are you in AA?

Black   No. No AA. I just quit. I've had a lots of friends was drinkers. Most of em, for that matter. Most of em dead, too.

White   From drinking.

Black   Well. From drinkin or from reasons that dont get too far from drinkin. Not too long ago I had a friend to get run down by a taxicab. Now where do you reckon he was goin? Drunk.

White   I dont know. Where was he going?

Black   Goin after more whiskey. Had plenty at the house. But a drunk is always afraid of runnin out.

White   Was he killed?

Black   I hope so. We buried him.

White   I suppose there's a moral to this story.

Black   Well, it's just a story about what you want and what you get. Pain and happiness. I'll tell you another one.

White   All right.

Black   One Sunday they's a bunch of us settin around at my house drinkin. Sunday mornin. Favorite time for drunks to get together and drink and I'll let you think about why that might be so. Well here come one of my buddies with this girl. Evelyn. And Evelyn was drunk when she got there but we fixed her a drink and directly Redge—my buddy—he goes back in the kitchen to get him a drink only now the bottle's gone. Well, Redge has been around a few drinkin people in his time so he commences to hunt for the bottle. Looks in all the cabinets and behind everthing. He cant find it but of course he knows what's happened to it so he comes back in and he sets down and he looks at Miss Evelyn settin there on the sofa. Drunk as a goat. And he says: Evelyn, where's the whiskey? And Evelyn, she goes: Ah ghaga baba lala ghaga. And he says: Evelyn, where did you put the whiskey? Ah lala bloggle blabla. And Redge is settin there and this is beginnin to piss him off just a little and he gets in her face and he goes: Ah loddle loddle blabble ghaga blabla and she says I hid it in the toilet.

White   That's pretty funny.

Black   I thought you might like that.

White   And is that where the whiskey was?

Black   Oh yeah. That's a favorite place for drunks to hide a bottle. But the point of course is that the drunk's concern aint that he's goin to die from drinkin—which he is. It's that he's goin to run out of whiskey fore he gets a chance to do it. Are you hungry? I can come back to this. I aint goin to lose my place.

White   I'm all right. Go ahead.

Black   If you was to hand a drunk a drink and tell him he really dont want it what do you reckon he'd say?

White   I think I know what he'd say.

Black   Sure you do. But you'd still be right.

White   About him not really wanting it.

Black   Yes. Because what he really wants he cant get. Or he thinks he cant get it. So what he really dont want he cant get enough of.

White   So what is it that he really wants.

Black   You know what he really wants.

White   No I dont.

Black   Yeah you do.

White   No I dont.

Black   Hm.

White   Hm what.

Black   You a hard case, Professor.

White   You're not exactly a day at the beach yourself.

Black   You dont know what he wants.

White   No. I do not.

Black   He wants what everbody wants.

White   And that is?

Black   He wants to be loved by God.

White   I dont want to be loved by God.

Black   I love that. See how you cut right to it? He dont either. Accordin to him. He just wants a drink of whiskey. You a smart man, Professor. You tell me which one makes sense and which one dont.

White   I dont want a drink of whiskey, either.

Black   I thought you just got done askin for one?

White   I mean as a general proposition.

Black   We aint talkin about no general propositions. We talkin about a drink.

White   I dont have a drinking problem.

Black   Well you got some kind of a problem.

White   Well whatever kind of a problem I have it's not something that I imagine can be addressed with a drink of liquor.

Black   Mm. I love the way you put that. So what can it be addressed with?

White   I think you know what it can be addressed with.

Black   The Sunset Limited.

White   Yes.

Black   And that's what you want.

White   That's what I want. Yes.

Black   That's a mighty big drink of whiskey, Professor.

White   That I dont really want.

Black   That you dont really want. Yes.

White   Well. I think I do want it.

Black   Of course you do, honey. If you didnt we wouldnt be settin here.

White   Well. I disagree with you.

Black   That's all right. That's the hand I'm playin.

White   I dont think you understand that people such as myself see a yearning for God as something lacking in those people.

Black   I do understand that. Couldnt agree more.

White   You agree with that?

Black   Sure I do. What's lackin is God.

White   Well, as I say, we'll just have to disagree.

Black   You aint closin down the forum for discussion are you?

White   Not at this juncture.

Black   Cause I had a little more to say.

White   How did I know that?

Black   I did go to one or two AA meetins. Lot of folks didnt like the God part of it all that much but I hadnt set there too long fore I figured out that the God part was really all the part they was. The problem wasnt that they was too much God in AA it was that they wasnt enough. And I got a pretty thick head about some things but I finally figured out that what was true about AA was probably true about a lot of other things too.

White   Well I'm sorry, but to me the whole idea of God is just a load of crap.

The black puts his hand to his chest and leans back.

Black   Oh Lord have mercy oh save us Jesus. The professor's done blasphemed all over us. We aint never gone be saved now.

He closes his eyes and shakes his head, laughing silently.

White   You dont find that an evil thing to say.

Black   Oh Mercy. No, Professor. I dont. But you does.

White   No I dont. It's simply a fact.

Black   No it aint no simply a fact. It's the biggest fact about you. It's just about the only fact.

White   But you dont seem to think that it's so bad.

Black   Well, I know it to be curable. So it aint *that* bad. If you talkin about what that man up there thinks about it I figure he's probably seen enough of it that it dont bother him as bad as you might think. I mean, what if somebody told you that you didnt exist. And you settin there listenin to him say it. That wouldnt really piss you off, would it?

White   No. You'd just feel sorry for them.

Black   I think that's right. You might even try to get
         some help for em. Now in my case he had to
         holler at me out loud and me layin on a slab in
         two pieces that they'd sewed back together
         where some nigger done tried to core me like a
         apple but still I got to say that if God is God
         then he can speak to your heart at any time and
         furthermore I got to say that if he spoke to
         me—which he did—then he can speak to any-
         body.

*The black drums his fingers lightly three times on the table
and looks at the professor.*

Silence.

Black   Well. Wonder what this crazy nigger fixin to do.
         He liable to put the mojo on me. Be speakin in
         tongues here directly. I better get my ass out of
         here. He's liable to try and steal my pocket-
         book. Need to get my ass down to the train
         depot fore somethin happen to me. What we
         goin to do with you, Professor?

White   I need to go.

Black   I thought you was goin to stay and visit with me
         some.

White   Look. I know I owe you a good deal. In the
         eyes of the world at least. Cant I just give you

something and we'll call it square? I could give you some money. Something like that.

The black studies him. He doesnt answer.

White   I could give you a thousand dollars. Well. That's not very much, I guess. I could give you three thousand, say.

Black   You dont have no notion the trouble you in, do you?

White   I dont know what you mean.

Black   I know you dont.

White   I'd just like to settle this someway.

Black   It aint me you got to settle with.

White   Do you really believe I was sent to you by God?

Black   Oh it's worse than that.

White   How do you mean?

Black   Belief aint like unbelief. If you a believer then you got to come finally to the well of belief itself and then you dont have to look no further.

There aint no further. But the unbeliever has got a problem. He has set out to unravel the world, but everthing he can point to that aint true leaves two new things layin there. If God walked the earth when he got done makin it then when you get up in the mornin you get to put your feet on a real floor and you dont have to worry about where it come from. But if he didnt then you got to come up with a whole other description of what you even mean by real. And you got to judge everthing by that same light. If light it is. Includin yourself. One question fits all. So what do you think, Professor? Is you real?

White   I'm not buying it.

Black   That's all right. It's been on the market a long time and it'll be there a while yet.

White   Do you believe everything that's in there? In the bible?

Black   The literal truth?

White   Yes.

Black   Probably not. But then you already know I'm a outlaw.

White   What is it you would disagree with?

Black   Maybe the notion of original sin. When Eve eat the apple and it turned everbody bad. I dont see people that way. I think for the most part people are good to start with. I think evil is somethin you bring on your own self. Mostly from wantin what you aint supposed to have. But I aint goin to set here and tell you about me bein a heretic when I'm tryin to get you to quit bein one.

White   Are you a heretic?

Black   You tryin to put me in the trick bag, Professor.

White   No I'm not. Are you?

Black   No more than what a man should be. Even a man with a powerful belief. I aint a doubter. But I am a questioner.

White   What's the difference?

Black   Well, I think the questioner wants the truth. The doubter wants to be told there aint no such thing.

White   *(Pointing at bible)* You dont think you have to believe everything in there in order to be saved?

Black   No. I dont. I dont think you even have to read it. I aint for sure you even got to know there is such a book. I think whatever truth is wrote in these pages is wrote in the human heart too and it was wrote there a long time ago and will still be wrote there a long time hence. Even if this book is burned ever copy of it. What Jesus said? I dont think he made up a word of it. I think he just told it. This book is a guide for the ignorant and the sick at heart. A whole man wouldnt need it at all. And of course if you read this book you goin to find that they's a lot more talk in here about the wrong way than they is about the right way. Now why is that?

White   I dont know. Why is it?

Black   I'd rather hear from you.

White   I'll have to think about it.

Black   Okay.

Silence.

White   Okay what?

Black   Okay go ahead and think about it.

White   It might take me a little longer than you to think about something.

Black   That's all right.

White   That's all right.

Black   Yes. I mean they's two ways you can take that remark but I'm goin to take it the good way. It's just my nature. That way I get to live in my world instead of yours.

White   What makes you think mine's so bad?

Black   Oh I dont know as it's so bad. I know it's brief.

White   All right. Are you ready?

Black   I'm ready.

White   I think the answer to your question is that the dialectic of the homily always presupposes a ground of evil.

Black   Man.

White   How's that.

Black   That's strong as a mare's breath, Professor. Wouldnt I love to lay some of that shit on the brothers? Whoa. Now. Just the two of us here talkin. In private. What did you just say?

White   Your question. The bible is full of cautionary tales. All of literature, for that matter. Telling us to be careful. Careful of what? Taking a wrong turn. A wrong path. How many wrong paths are there? Their number is legion. How many right paths? Only one. Hence the imbalance you spoke of.

Black   Man. I'll tell you what, Professor. You could go on television. Goodlookin man such as yourself. Did you know that?

White   Stop.

Black   I'm serious. I wasnt even all that sure you *was* a professor till you laid that shit on me.

White   I think you're having fun at my expense.

Black   Aint done no such a thing, Professor.

White   Well. I think you are.

Black   Honey, I swear I aint. I couldnt say a thing like you just got done sayin. I admire that.

White   And why do you keep calling me honey?

Black   That's just the old south talkin. They aint nothin wrong with it. I'll try and quit if it bothers you.

White   I'm just not sure what it means.

Black   It means you among friends. It means quit worryin bout everthing.

White   That might be easier said than done.

Black   Well yes it might. But we just talkin here. Just talkin.

White   What else?

Black   What else what?

White   Any other heresies?

Black   At this juncture?

White   At this juncture. Yes.

Black   Yeah, but I aint tellin you.

White   Why not?

Black   Cause I aint. Shouldnt of told you what I did.

White   Why not?

Black   You settin here at my table dead to God as the fallen angels and you waitin on me to lay another heresy on you to clutch to your bosom and help shore you up in your infidelity and I aint goin to do it. That's all.

White   Dont then.

Black   Dont worry. I aint.

White   I have to go.

Black   Ever time the dozens gets a little heavy you got to go.

White   What's the dozens?

Black   It aint really even the dozens. It's really just a discussion.

White   What's the dozens.

Black   It's when two of the brothers stands around insultin one another and the first one gets pissed off loses.

White   What is the point of it?

Black   Winnin and losin is the point of it. Same as the point of everthing else.

White   And you win by making the other guy angry.

Black   That's correct.

White   I dont get it.

Black   You aint supposed to get it. You *white*.

White   Then why did you tell me?

Black   Cause you asked me.

White   So if I find you a bit irritating and decide to leave then I lose.

Black   Well, like I said, this aint even the dozens. We just talkin.

White   But that's what you think.

Black   Oh yeah, that's what I think.

White   Well how long do you think I might have to stay before I could leave without losing?

Black   That's kindly hard to say. I guess the best way to put it might be that you'd have to stay till you didnt want to leave.

White   Stay until I didnt want to leave.

Black   Yeah.

White   And then I could leave.

Black   Yeah.

The professor runs one hand alongside his head and then holds the back of his neck, his head down and his eyes closed. He looks up.

White Why is it called the dozens?

Black Dont know.

White What sorts of insults?

Black Oh, you might say somethin about the other man's mama. That's a sensitive area, you might say. And he might lose it and come after your ass but when he done that it's like he's sayin that what you just got done tellin about his mama was true. It's like he sayin: You aint supposed to know that about my mama and you damn sure aint supposed to of told it and now I'm fixin to whip your ass. You see what I'm sayin?

White I suppose.

Black Well, probably not.

White And is this something you do with your friends?

Black Me? No. I dont play the dozens.

White Tell me something.

Black   Sure.

White   Why are you here? What do you get out of this? You seem like a smart man.

Black   Me? I'm just a dumb country nigger from Louisiana. I done told you. I aint never had the first thought in my head. If it aint in here then I dont know it.

He holds the bible up off the table and lays it down again.

White   Half the time I think you're having fun with me. I dont see how you can live here. I dont see how you can feel safe.

Black   Well you got a point, Professor. About bein safe anyways.

White   Have you ever stopped any of these people from taking drugs?

Black   Not that I know of.

White   Then what is the point? I dont get it. I mean, it's hopeless. This place is just a moral leper colony.

Black   Damn, Professor. Moral leper colony? Where my pencil at?

He pretends to rummage through the kitchen table drawer.

White   Well it is.

Black   I aint never goin to want you to leave. Put that in my book.

White   In your book?

Black   *In the Moral Leper Colony.* Damn, I like the sound of that.

White   You're kidding me.

Black   You know I aint writin no book.

White   Well I still dont get it. Why not go someplace where you might be able to do some good?

Black   As opposed to someplace where good was needed.

White   Even God gives up at some point. There's no ministry in hell. That I ever heard of.

Black   No there aint. That's well put. Ministry is for the livin. That's why you responsible for your brother. Once he's quit breathin you cant help him no more. After that he's in the hands of other parties. So you got to look after him now. You might even want to monitor his train schedule.

White   You think you are your brother's keeper.

Black   I dont believe *think* quite says it.

White   And Jesus is a part of this enterprise.

Black   Is that okay with you?

White   And he's interested in coming here to this cesspool and salvaging what everybody knows is unsalvageable. Why would he do that? You said he didnt have a lot of free time. Why would he come here? What would be the difference to him between a building that was morally and spiritually vacant and one that was just plain empty?

Black   Mm. Professor you a theologian here and I didnt even know it.

White   You're being facetious.

Black   I dont know that word. Dont be afraid to talk down to me. You aint goin to hurt my feelins.

77

White   It means. I guess it means that you're not being sincere. That you dont mean what you're saying. In a cynical sort of way.

Black   Mm. You think I dont mean what I'm sayin.

White   Sometimes. I think you say things for effect.

Black   Mm. Well, let me say this for effect.

White   Go ahead.

Black   Suppose I was to tell you that if you could bring yourself to unlatch your hands from around your brother's throat you could have life everlastin?

White   There's no such thing. Everybody dies.

Black   That aint what he said. He said you could have *life* everlastin. Life. Have it today. Hold it in your hand. That you could see it. It gives off a light. It's got a little weight to it. Not much. Warm to the touch. Just a little. And it's forever. And you can have it. Now. Today. But you dont want it. You dont want it cause to get it you got to let you brother off the hook. You got to actually take him and hold him in your arms and it dont make no difference what color he is or what he smells like or even if he dont want to *be* held. And the *reason* you wont do it is because he dont deserve it. And about that there aint no argument. He *dont* deserve it. *(He leans forward, slow and deliberate.)* You wont do it because it aint just. Aint that so?

Silence.

Black   Aint it?

White   I dont believe in those sorts of things.

Black   Just answer the question Professor.

White   I dont think in those terms.

Black   I know you dont. Answer the question.

White   I suppose there's some truth in what you say.

Black   But that's all I'm goin to get.

White   Yes.

Black   Well. That's all right. I'll take it. Some is a lot. We down to breadcrumbs here.

White   I really have to go.

Black   Just stay. Just a little. We can talk bout somethin else. You like baseball? Tell you what. Why dont I fix us somethin to eat?

White   I'm not hungry.

Black   How about some coffee then?

White   All right. But then I've got to go.

Black   *(Rising)* All right. The man says all right.

He runs water in the kettle at the sink and pours the water into the percolator.

Black   You see I wouldnt be this rude under normal circumstances. Man come in my house and set at my table and me not offer him nothin? But with you I figure I got to strategize. Got to play my cards right. Keep you from slippin off into the night.

He spoons coffee from a can into the percolator and plugs the percolator in.

White   It's not night.

Black   Depends on what kind of night we talkin bout.

He comes back to the table and sits.

Black   Let me ask you kindly a personal question.

White   This will be good.

Black   What do *you* think is wrong with you that has finally narrowed all your choices down to the Sunset Limited?

White   I dont think there's anything wrong with me. I think I've just been driven to finally face the truth. If I'm different it doesnt mean I'm crazy.

Black   Different.

White   Yes.

Black   Different from who?

White   From anybody.

Black   What about them other folks tryin to off they-selves?

White   What about them?

Black   Well, maybe them is the folks that you is like. Maybe them folks is your natural kin. Only you all just dont get together all that much.

White   I dont think so.

Black   Dont think so.

White   No. I've been in group therapy with those people. I never found anyone there that I felt any kinship with.

Black   What about them other professors? They aint no kinship there?

White   (*Disgustedly*) Good god.

Black   I'm goin to take that for a no.

White   I loathe them and they loathe me.

Black   Well now wait a minute. Just cause you dont like em dont mean you *aint* like em. What was that word? Loathe?

White   Loathe.

Black   That's a pretty powerful word, aint it?

White   Not powerful enough, I'm afraid.

Black   So how come you be loathin these other pro-
          fessors?

White   I know what you're thinking.

Black   What am I thinkin?

White   You're thinking that I loathe them because I'm
          like them and I loathe myself.

Black   (*Sitting back in his chair*) Damn, Professor. If I
          had your brains aint no tellin what all I might
          of done. I'd of been a drug king or somethin.
          Ride round in a Rolls Royce.

White   You're being facetious again.

Black   No I aint. I wasnt the first time. Let me ask you
          this.

White   All right.

Black   Is you on any kind of medication?

White   No.

Black   They aint got no medication for pilgrims waitin
          to take the Sunset?

White   For suicidal depression.

Black   Yeah.

White   Yes. They do. I've tried them.

Black   And what happened?

White   Nothing happened.

Black   You didnt get no relief.

White   No. I think the coffee's percolated.

Black   I know. Does these drugs work for most folks?

White   Yes. For most.

Black   But not for you.

White   Not for me. No.

Black   *(Rising)* And what do you make of that?

White   I dont know. What am I supposed to make of it?

Black   *(Crossing to kitchen counter)* I dont know, Professor. I just tryin to find you some constituents out there somewheres.

White   Constituents?

Black   (*Unplugging percolator and getting down cups*)
Yeah. You like that?

White   Is that a word they use on the streets?

Black   Naw. I learned that word in the jailhouse. You
pick up stuff from these jailhouse lawyers and
then it gets used around. Be talkin bout your
constituents. Some other cat's constituents. Your
wife's constituents. You use cream and sugar?

White   No. Just *black*.

Black   Just *black*.

White   Why do I have to have constituents?

Black   I aint said you *got* to. I just wondered if maybe
you do and we just aint looked hard enough.

He brings the percolator and the cups to the table and pours.

Black   They could be out there. Maybe they's some
other drugproof terminal commuters out there
that could be your friends.

White   Terminal commuters?

Black   Got a nice sound to it, aint it?

White   It's all right.

Black   (*Sitting*) Nobody.

White   Nobody. No.

Black   Hm.

White   I'm not a member. I never wanted to be. I never was.

Black   Not a member.

White   No.

Black   Well. Sometimes people dont know what they want till they get it.

White   Maybe. But I think they know what they dont want.

Black   I dont know, Professor. I try and go by what I see. The simplest things has got more to em than you can ever understand. Bunch of people standin around on a train platform of a mornin. Waitin to go to work. Been there a hundred times. A thousand maybe. It's just a train platform. Aint nothin else much you can say about it. But they might be one commuter waitin there on the edge of that platform that for him it's somethin else. It might even be the edge of the world. The edge of the universe. He's starin at the end of all tomorrows and he's drawin a shade over ever yesterday that ever was. So he's a different kind of commuter. He's worlds away from them everday travelers. Nothin to do with them at all. Well. Is that right?

White   I dont know.

Black   I know you dont. Bless your heart. I know you dont.

They sip their coffee.

Black   You ride that subway ever day, Professor?

White   Yes.

Black   What do you think about them people?

White   On the subway?

Black   On the subway.

White   I try not to think about them at all.

Black   You ever speak to any of em?

White	Speak to them?
Black	Yeah.
White	About what?
Black	About anything.
White	No. God no.
Black	God no?
White	Yes. God no.
Black	You ever curse em?
White	Curse them?
Black	Yeah.
White	Why would I do that?
Black	I dont know. Do you?
White	No. Of course not.
Black	I mean where they cant hear it.
White	What do you mean?
Black	Maybe just under your breath. In your heart. To yourself.

White   Because?

Black   I dont know. Maybe they just in your way. Or you dont like the way they look. The way they smell. What they doin.

White   And I would mutter something ugly under my breath.

Black   Yeah.

White   I suppose.

Black   And how often do you reckon you might do that?

White   You really dont get to interrogate me, you know.

Black   I know. How often?

White   I dont know. With some frequency. Probably.

Black   Give me a number.

White   A number?

Black   Yeah. Say just on a average day.

White   I've no idea.

Black   Sure you do.

White   A number.

Black   I'm a number man.

White   Two or three times a day, I would guess. Something like that. Maybe.

Black   Could be more.

White   Oh yes.

Black   Could be five?

White   Probably.

Black   Ten?

White   That might be a bit high.

Black   But we can go with five. That's safe.

White   Yes.

Black   That's eighteen twenty-five. Can we round that off to two grand?

White   What's that, per year?

Black   Yeah.

White   Two thousand? That's a lot.

Black   Yes it is. But is it accurate?

White   I suppose. So?

Black   So. I aint goin to guess your age but let me put you on the low side and say times twenty years of commutin and now we got forty thousand curses heaped on the heads of folks you dont even know.

White   So where is this going?

Black   I just wondered if you ever thought about that. If it might have anything to do with the shape you has managed to get yourself in.

White   It's just symptomatic of the larger issues. I dont like people.

Black   But you wouldnt hurt them people.

White   No. Of course not.

Black   You sure.

White   Of course I'm sure. Why would I hurt them?

Black   I dont know. Why would you hurt yourself?

White   It's not the same thing.

Black   You sure about that?

White   I'm not them and they're not me. I think I know the difference.

Black   Mm.

White   More mm's.

Black   You sure you aint hungry?

White   No.

Black   You aint eat nothin.

White   That's all right.

Black   I see you eyein the door. I got to strategize, you know.

White   I'm really not hungry.

Black   Active morning like you had you aint worked up no appetite?

White   No.

Black   I see you lookin around. Everthing in here is clean. No, dont say nothin. It's all right.

The black pushes back his chair and rises.

Black   I could eat a bite and I think you could too.

The black goes to the refrigerator and takes out some pots. He turns on the stove. He washes his hands and dries them with a towel.

Black   You break bread with a man you have moved on to another level of friendship. I heard somewheres that that's true the world over.

White   Probably.

Black   I like probably. Probably from you is worth a couple of damn rights anywheres else.

White   Why? Because I dont believe in anything?

The black has put the pots on the stove to warm and he brings napkins and silverware to the table and sets them out. He sits down.

Black   Well. I dont think that's the problem. I think it's what you do believe that is carryin you off, not what you dont. Let me ask you this.

White   Go ahead.

Black   You ever think about Jesus?

White   Here we go.

Black   Do you?

White   What makes you think I'm not jewish?

Black   What, jews aint allowed to think about Jesus?

White   No, but they might think about him differently.

Black   Is you jewish?

White   No. As it happens. I'm not.

Black   Whew. You had me worried there for a minute.

White   What, you dont like jews?

Black   *(Shaking his head, almost laughing)* Pullin your chain, Professor. Pullin your chain. I dont know why I love to mess with you. But I do. You need to listen. Or you need to believe what you hearin. The whole point of where this is goin—which you wanted to know—is that they aint no jews. Aint no *white*s. Aint no niggers.

People of color. Aint none of that. At the deep bottom of the mine where the gold is at there aint none of that. There's just the pure ore. That forever thing. That you dont think is there. That thing that helps to keep folks nailed down to the platform when the Sunset Limited comes through. Even when they think they might want to get aboard. That thing that makes it possible to ladle out benediction upon the heads of strangers instead of curses. It's all the same thing. And it aint but one thing. Just one.

White   And that would be Jesus.

Black   Got to think about how to answer that. Maybe one more heresy wont hurt you. You pretty loaded up on em already. Here's what I would say. I would say that the thing we are talkin about is Jesus, but it is Jesus understood as that gold at the bottom of the mine. He couldnt come down here and take the form of a man if that form was not done shaped to accommodate him. And if I said that there aint no way for Jesus to be ever man without ever man bein Jesus then I believe that might be a pretty big heresy. But that's all right. It aint as big a heresy as sayin that a man aint all that much different from a rock. Which is how your view looks to me.

White   It's not my view. I believe in the primacy of the intellect.

Black   What is that word.

White   Primacy? It means first. It means what you put first.

Black   And that would be intellect.

White   Yes.

Black   What about the primacy of the Sunset Limited?

White   Yes. That too.

Black   But not the primacy of all them folks waitin on a later train.

White   No. No primacy there.

Black   Mm.

White   Mm what.

Black   You tough, Professor. You tough.

The black rises and goes to the stove. He reaches down plates and stirs the pots and ladles out the dinner. He takes

*down a loaf of white bread and puts four slices on a plate
and brings the plate of bread to the table and sets it down.*

Black   Yeah you tough.

*The black brings the two plates to the table and sets them
out and takes his seat. He looks at the professor.*

Black   You see yourself as a questioner, Professor. But
           about that I got my doubts. Even so, the quest
           of your life is *your* quest. You on a road that
           you laid. And that fact alone might be all the
           reason you need for keepin to it. As long as you
           on that road you cant be lost.

White   I'm not sure I understand what you're saying.

Black   Well, Professor. I have got some very serious
           doubts about you not understandin anything I
           say. Now I'm goin to say Grace.

*The black puts his hands on the table at either side of his
plate and bows his head.*

Black   Lord we thank you for this food and we ask
           that you keep us ever mindful of the many

blessins we have received from your hand. We thank you today for the life of the professor that you have returned to us and we ask that you continue to look after him because we need him. *(Pause)* I aint sure why we need him. I just know we do. Amen.

The black looks up. He smiles at the professor.

Black All right. You tell me if you like this.

White It looks good.

They begin to eat.

White This is good.

They eat.

White This is very good.

Black Supposed to be good. This is soul food, my man.

White   It's got what in it? Molasses?

Black   Mm. You a chef, Professor?

White   Not really.

Black   But some.

White   Some, yes. Bananas, of course. Mangos?

Black   Got a mango or two in there. Rutabagas.

White   Rutabagas?

Black   Rutabagas. *Them* aint easy to find.

White   It's very good.

Black   It gets better after a day or two. I just fixed this last night. You need to warm it up a few times to get the flavors right.

White   Like chile.

Black   Like chile. That's right. You know where I learned to fix this?

White   In Louisana?

Black   Right here in the ghettos of New York City.
They's a lot of influences in a dish like this. You
got many parts of the world in that pot yonder.
Different countries. Different people.

White   Any *white* people?

Black   Not if you can help it.

White   Really?

Black   Messin with you, Professor. Messin with you.
You know these French chefs in these uptown
restaurants?

White   Not personally.

Black   You know what they like to cook?

White   No.

Black   Sweetbreads. Tripe. Brains. All that shit they
dont nobody eat. You know why that is?

White   Because it's a challenge? You have to innovate?

Black   You pretty smart for a cracker. A challenge.
That's right. The stuff they cook is dead cheap.
Most folks throws it out. Give it to the cat. But
poor folks dont throw nothin out.

White   I guess that's right.

Black   It dont take a lot of skill to make a porterhouse steak taste good. But what if you cant buy no porterhouse steak? You still wants to eat somethin that tastes good. What you do then?

White   Innovate.

Black   Innovate. That's right, Professor. And when do you innovate?

White   When you dont have something that you want.

Black   You fixin to get a A plus. So who would that be? That aint got what they want?

White   Poor people.

Black   I love this man. So how you like this?

White   It's very good.

Black   Well let me have your plate.

White   Just a small portion.

Black   That's all right, Professor. You need to eat. You done had yourself a pretty busy day.

*The black puts more of the dish on the professor's plate
and comes to the table and sets it in front of him.*

Black   You want some more coffee?

White   Yes. That would be great.

*He brings the pot to the table and pours his cup and sets the
pot on the table and takes his seat and they continue to eat.*

White   You dont think a glass of wine would have been
good with this?

Black   Oh no. I think it might of been good.

White   But you wouldnt drink it.

Black   Oh I might. One glass.

White   Jesus drank wine. He and his disciples.

Black   Yes he did. Accordin to the bible. Of course it
dont say nothin about him hidin it in the toilet.

White   Is that really a favorite hiding place?

Black   Oh yes. I've knowed drunks to lift the tops off
of toilet tanks in strange places just on the off
chance.

White   Is that true?

Black   Naw. It could be, though. Wouldnt surprise me none.

White   What is the worst thing you ever did.

Black   More jailhouse stories.

White   Why not?

Black   Which why not you want to hear?

White   Is bludgeoning the man in the prison cafeteria the worst thing you ever did?

Black   No. It aint.

White   Really? What's the worst?

Black   Aint goin tell you.

White   Why not?

Black   Cause you'd jump up and run out the door hollerin.

White   It must be pretty bad.

Black   It is pretty bad. That's why I aint tellin you.

White   Now I'm afraid to ask.

Black   No you aint.

White   Have you ever told anyone?

Black   Oh yeah. It wouldnt leave me alone. The soul might be silent but the servant of the soul has always got a voice and it has got one for a reason. The life of the master depends on the servant and this is one master that has got to be sustained. Got to be sustained.

White   Who did you tell it to?

Black   I told it to a man of God who was my friend.

White   What did he say?

Black   He didnt say a word.

White   But you're not curious about the worst thing I ever did.

Black   Yeah I am.

White   But you wont ask me what it is.

Black   Dont have to.

White   Why is that?

Black   Cause I was there and I seen it.

White   Well, I might have a different view.

Black   Yeah. You might. You want some more?

White   No. I'm stuffed.

Black   Hungrier than you thought.

White   Yes. I was.

Black   Good.

White   Is this some kind of a test of your faith?

Black   What, you?

White   Me. Yes.

Black   Naw, Professor. It aint my faith you testin.

White   You see everything in *black* and *white*.

Black   It is *black* and *white*.

White   I suppose that makes the world easier to understand.

Black   You might be surprised about how little time I
            spend trying to understand the world.

White   You try to understand God.

Black   No I dont. I just try and understand what he
            wants from me.

White   And that is everything you need.

Black   If God aint everthing you need you in a world
            of trouble. And if what you sayin is that my
            view of the world is a narrow one I dont dis-
            agree with that. Of course I could point out
            that I aint down on the platform in my leapin
            costume.

White   You could.

Black   A lot of things is beyond my understandin. I
            know that. I say it again. If it aint in this book
            then they's a good chance that I dont know it.
            Before I started readin the bible I was pretty
            much in that primacy thing myself.

White   Primacy thing.

Black   Yeah. Not as bad as you. But pretty bad. I was
            pretty dumb, but I wasnt dumb enough to
            believe that what had got me nowheres in forty

years was all of a sudden goin to get me somewheres. I was dumb, but I wasnt that dumb. I
seen what was there for the askin, and I
decided to ask. And that's all I done. And it was
hard. I'll tell you right now, Professor, it was
hard. I was layin there all cut up and chained to
that hospital bed and I was cryin I hurt so bad
and I thought they'd kill me if I did live and I
tried to say it and tried to say it and after a
while I just quit. I put all of that away from me.
And I just said it. I said: Please help me. And
he did.

They sit.

Black   Long silence.

White   It's just a silence.

Black   Well. That's my story, Professor. It's easy told. I
dont make a move without Jesus. When I get
up in the mornin I just try to get ahold of his
belt. Oh, ever once in a while I'll catch myself
slippin into manual override. But I catch
myself. I catch myself.

White   Manual override?

Black   You like that?

White   It's okay.

Black   I thought it was pretty good.

White   So you come to the end of your rope and you admit defeat and you are in despair and in this state you seize upon this whatever it is that has neither substance nor sense and you grab hold of it and hang on for dear life. Is that a fair portrayal?

Black   Well, that could be one way to say it.

White   It doesnt make any sense.

Black   Well, I thought when we was talkin earlier I heard you to say they wasnt none of it made no sense. Talkin bout the history of the world and all such as that.

White   It doesnt. On a larger scale. But what you're telling me isnt a view of things. It's a view of one thing. And I find it nonsensical.

Black   What would you do if Jesus was to speak to you?

White   Why? Do you imagine that he might?

Black   No. I dont. But I dont know.

White   I'm not virtuous enough.

Black   No, Professor, it aint nothin like that. You dont have to be virtuous. You just has to be quiet. I cant speak for the Lord but the experience I've had leads me to believe that he'll speak to anybody that'll listen. You damn sure aint got to be virtuous.

White   Well if I heard God talking to me, then I'd be ready for you to take me up to Bellevue. As you suggested.

Black   What if what he said made sense?

White   It wouldnt make any difference. Craziness is craziness.

Black   Dont make no difference if it makes sense.

White   No.

Black   Mm. Well, that's about as bad a case of the primacy as I ever heard.

White   Well. I've always gone my own way. Ich kann nicht anders.

Black   What is that you talkin?

White   It's german.

Black   You talk german?

White   Not really. A little. It's a quotation.

Black   Didnt do them Germans much good though, did it?

White   I dont know. The Germans contributed a great deal to civilization. (*Pause*) Before Hitler.

Black   And then they contributed Hitler.

White   If you like.

Black   Wasnt none of my doin.

White   I gather it to be your belief that culture tends to contribute to human misery. That the more one knows the more unhappy one is likely to be.

Black   As in the case of certain parties known to us.

White   As in the case.

Black   I dont believe I said that. In fact, I think maybe you said it.

White   I never said it.

Black   Mm. But do you believe it?

White   No.

Black   No?

White   I dont know. It could be true.

Black   Well why is that? It dont seem right, does it?

White   It's the first thing in that book there. The Garden of Eden. Knowledge as destructive to the spirit. Destructive to goodness.

Black   I thought you aint read this book?

White   Everyone knows that story. It's probably the most famous story in there.

Black   So why do you think that is?

White   I suppose from the God point of view all knowledge is vanity. Or maybe it gives people the unhealthy illusion that they can outwit the devil.

Black   Damn, Professor. Where was you when I needed you?

White You'd better be careful. You see where it's gotten me.

Black I do see. It's the subject at hand.

White The darker picture is always the correct one. When you read the history of the world you are reading a saga of bloodshed and greed and folly the import of which is impossible to ignore. And yet we imagine that the future will somehow be different. I've no idea why we are even still here but in all probability we will not be here much longer.

Black Them is some pretty powerful words, Professor. That's what's in your heart, aint it?

White Yes.

Black Well I can relate to them thoughts.

White You can?

Black Yes I can.

White That surprises me. What, you're going to think about them?

Black I done have thought about em. I've thought about em for a long time. Not as good as you said it. But pretty close.

White   Well you surprise me. And you've come to what conclusions?

Black   I aint. I'm still thinkin.

White   Yes. Well, I'm not.

Black   Things can change.

White   No they cant.

Black   You could be wrong.

White   I dont think so.

Black   But that aint somethin you have a lot of in your life.

White   What isnt?

Black   Bein wrong.

White   I admit it when I'm wrong.

Black   I dont think so.

White   Well, you're entitled to your opinion.

The black leans back and regards the professor. He reaches and picks up the newspaper from the table and leans back again and adjusts his glasses.

Black   Let's see here. Story on page three.

He folds the paper elaborately.

Black   Yeah. Here it is. Friends report that the man had ignored all advice and had stated that he intended to pursue his own course.

He adjusts his glasses.

Black   A close confidant stated *(he looks up)*—and this here is a quotation—said: You couldnt tell the son of a bitch nothin. *(He looks up again)* Can you say that in the papers? Son of a bitch? Meanwhile, bloodspattered spectators at the hundred and fifty-fifth street station—continued on page four.

He wets his thumb and laboriously turns the page and refolds the paper.

Black   —who were interviewed at the scene all reported that the man's last words as he hurtled toward the oncomin commuter train were: I am right.

He lays down the paper and adjusts his spectacles and peers over the top of them at the professor.

White   Very funny.

The black takes off his glasses and lowers his head and pinches the bridge of his nose and shakes his head.

Black   Oh Professor. Mm. You an amazin man.

White   I'm glad you find me entertaining.

Black   Well, you pretty special.

White   I dont think I'm special.

Black   You dont.

White   No. I dont.

Black   You dont think you might view them other commuters from a certain height?

White   I view those other commuters as fellow occupants of the same abyssal pit in which I find myself. If they see it as something else I dont know how that makes me special.

Black   Mm. I hear what you sayin. But still I keep
        comin back to them commuters. Them that's
        waitin on the Sunset? I got to think maybe they
        could be just a little bit special theyselves. I
        mean, they got to be in a deeper pit than just
        us daytravelers. A deeper and a darker. I aint
        sayin they down as deep as you, but pretty
        deep maybe.

White   So?

Black   So how come they cant be your brothers in
        despair and selfdestruction? I thought misery
        loved company?

White   I'm sure I don't know.

Black   Well let me take a shot at it.

White   Be my guest.

Black   What I think is that you got better reasons then
        them. I mean, their reasons is just that they
        dont like it here, but yours says what they is not
        to like and why not to like it. You got more
        intelligent reasons. More elegant reasons.

White   Are you making fun of me?

Black   No. I aint.

White   But you think I'm full of shit.

Black   I dont think that. Oh I dont doubt but what it's possible to die from bein full of shit. But I dont think that's what we lookin at here.

White   What do you think we're looking at?

Black   I dont know. You got me on unfamiliar ground. You got these elegant world class reasons for takin the Limited and these other dudes all they got is maybe they just dont feel good. In fact, it might could be that you aint even all that unhappy.

White   You think that my education is driving me to suicide.

Black   Well, no. I'm just posin the question. Wait a minute. Fore you answer.

He takes his pad and his pencil and begins to write laboriously, his tongue in the corner of his mouth, grimacing. This for the professor's benefit. He looks sideways at him and smiles. He tears off the page and folds it and puts it in his shirtpocket.

Black   All right. Go ahead.

White   I think that's the most ridiculous thing I ever heard.

The black takes the folded paper from his pocket and hands it across. The professor opens it and reads it aloud.

White   I think that's the most ridiculous thing I ever heard. Very clever. What's the point?

Black   The point dont change. The point is always the same point. It's what I said before and what I keep lookin for ways to say it again. The light is all around you, cept you dont see nothin but shadow. And the shadow is you. You the one makin it.

White   Well, I dont have your faith. Why dont we just leave it at that.

Black   You dont never think about maybe just startin over?

White   I did. At one time. I dont any more.

Black   Sometimes faith might just be a case of not havin nothin else left.

White   Well, I do have something else.

Black   Maybe you could just keep that in reserve.
          Maybe just take a shot at startin over. I dont
          mean start again. Everbody's done that. Over
          means over. It means you just walk away. I
          mean, if everthing you are and everthing you
          have and everthing you have done has brought
          you at last to the bottom of a whiskey bottle or
          bought you a one way ticket on the Sunset
          Limited then you cant give me the first reason
          on God's earth for salvagin none of it. Cause
          they aint no reason. And I'm goin to tell you
          that if you can bring yourself to shut the door
          on all of that it will be cold and it will be lonely
          and they'll be a mean wind blowin. And them is
          all good signs. You dont say nothin. You just
          turn up your collar and keep walkin.

White   I cant.

Black   Yeah.

White   I cant.

Black   You want some more coffee?

White   No. Thank you.

Black   Why do you think folks takes their own lives?

White   I dont know. Different reasons.

Black   Yeah. But is there somethin them different reasons has got in common?

White   I cant speak for others. My own reasons center around a gradual loss of make-believe. That's all. A gradual enlightenment as to the nature of reality. Of the world.

Black   Them worldly reasons.

White   If you like.

Black   Them elegant reasons.

White   That was your description.

Black   You didnt disagree with it.

The professor shrugs.

Black   It's them reasons that your brother dont know nothin about hangin by his necktie from the steampipe down in the basement. He got his own dumb-ass reasons, but maybe if we could educate him to where some of them more elegant reasons was available to him and his buddies then they'd be a lot of folks out there could off theyselves with more joy in they hearts. What do you think?

White   Now I know you're being facetious.

Black   This time I think you're right. I think you have finally drove me to it.

White   Mm hm.

Black   Well, the professor's done gone to layin the mm hm's on me. I better watch my step.

White   Yes you had. I might be warming up the trick bag.

Black   But still you think that your reasons is about the world and his is mostly just about him.

White   I think that's probably true.

Black   I see a different truth. Settin right across the table from me.

White   Which is?

Black   That you must love your brother or die.

White   I dont know what that means. That's another world from anything I know.

Black   What's the world you know.

White   You dont want to hear.

Black   Sure I do.

White   I dont think so.

Black   Go ahead.

White   All right. It's that the world is basically a forced labor camp from which the workers—perfectly innocent—are led forth by lottery, a few each day, to be executed. I dont think that this is just the way I see it. I think it's the way it is. Are there alternate views? Of course. Will any of them stand close scrutiny? No.

Black   Man.

White   So. Do you want to take a look at that train schedule again?

Black   And they aint nothin to be done about it.

White   No. The efforts that people undertake to improve the world invariably make it worse. I used to think there were exceptions to that dictum. I dont think that now.

The black sits back, looking down at the table. He shakes his head slightly.

White   What else do you want to talk about?

Black   I dont know. Them sounds to me like the words of a man on his way to the train station.

White   They are those words.

Black   What do you think about that man?

White   I'm like you. I dont. I used to. Now I dont. I think about minimalizing pain. That is my life. I dont know why it isnt everyone's.

Black   You dont think gettin run over by a train might smart just a little?

White   No. I did the calculations. At seventy miles an hour the train is outrunning the neurons. It should be totally painless.

Black   I'm goin to be stuck with your ass for a while, aint I?

White   I hope not.

Black   If this aint the life you had in mind, what was?

White   I dont know. Not this. Is your life the one you'd planned?

Black   No, it aint. I got what I needed instead of what I wanted and that's just about the best kind of luck you can have.

White   Yes. Well.

Black   You cant compare your life to mine, can you?

White   In all honesty, no. I cant.

Black   Mm.

White   I'm sorry. I should go.

Black   You dont have to go.

White   I've offended you.

Black   I got a thicker hide than that, Professor. Just stay. You aint hurt my feelins.

White   I know you think that I should be thankful and I'm sorry not to be.

Black   Now Professor, I dont think no such a thing.

White   I should go.

Black   I'm diggin a dry hole here, aint I?

White   I admire your persistence.

Black   What can I do to get you to stay a bit?

White   Why? Are you hoping that if I stay long enough God might speak to me?

Black   No, I'm hopin he might speak to me.

White   I know you think I at least owe you a little more of my time. I know I'm ungrateful. But ingratitude is not the sin to a spiritual bankrupt that it is to a man of God.

Black   You dont owe me nothin, Professor.

White   Do you really think that?

Black   Yes. I really do.

White   Well. You're very kind. I wish there was something I could do to repay you but there isnt. So why dont we just say goodbye and you can get on with your life.

Black   I cant.

White   You cant?

Black   No.

White   What do you want me to do?

Black   I dont know. Suppose you could wake up tomorrow and you wouldnt be wantin to jump in front of no train. Suppose all you had to do was ask. Would you do it?

White   It would depend on what I had to give up.

Black   I started to write that down and put it in my pocket.

White   What is it that you think I'm holding on to? What is it that the terminal commuter cherishes that he would die for?

Black   I dont know. I dont know.

White   No.

Black   You dont want to talk to me no more, do you?

White   I thought you had a thick skin.

Black   It's pretty thick. It aint hide to the bone.

White   *Why* do you think it? Why do you think there is
something?

Black   I dont know. It just seems to me that a man
that cant wait for a train to run over him has
got to have *somethin* on his mind. Most folks
would settle for maybe just a slap up the side of
the head. You say you dont care about nothin
but I dont believe that. I dont believe that
death is ever about nothin. You asked me what
I thought it was you was holdin on to and I got
to say I dont know. Or maybe I just dont have
the words to say it. And maybe you know but
you aint sayin. But I believe that when you took
your celebrated leap you was holdin on to it
and takin it with you. Holdin on for grim death.
I look for the words, Professor. I look for the
words because I believe that the words is the
way to your heart.

White   You think that anyone in my position is auto-
matically blind to the workings of his own
psyche.

Black   I think that anybody in your position is auto-
matically blind. But that aint the whole story.
Because we still talkin bout the rest of them

third railers and them takin one train and you takin another.

White   I didnt say that.

Black   Sure you did. They got a train for all them dumb-ass crackers that just feels bad and then they got this other train for you cause your pain and the world's pain is the same pain and this train requires a observation car and a diner.

White   Well. You can think what you want. You dont need my agreement.

Black   I know. But that aint the way to the trick bag.

White   Well. The trick bag seems to have shaped itself up into some sort of communal misery wherein one finds salvation by consorting among the loathsome.

Black   Damn, Professor. You puttin me in the bag. Where you come up with stuff like that?

White   It was phrased especially for you. For your enjoyment. You see what a whore I am?

Black   No you aint. You a smart man. Too smart for me.

White   I feel the bag yawning.

Black   I wish I knew how.

White   Do you really think that? That I'm too smart for you?

Black   Yes I do. If you can jack you own self around nine ways from Sunday I'd like to know what chance you think I got.

White   I see.

Black   What I need to do here is to buy more time. But I dont know what to buy it with.

White   You dont know what to offer a man about to board the Limited.

Black   No, I dont. I feel like I'm about traded out.

White   Maybe you are. Have you ever dealt with suicides?

Black   No. You the first one. These junkies and crack-heads is about as far from suicide as you can get. They wouldnt even know what you was talkin about. They wake up in pain ever day. Bad pain. But they aint headed for the depot. Now you can say, well, they got a fix for their pain. Just need to hustle on out there and get it. And that's a good argument. But still we got this question. Just what is this pain that is causin these express riders to belly up at the kiosk with the *black* crepe. What kind of pain we talkin about? I got to say that if it was grief that brought folks to suicide it'd be a full time job just to get em all in the ground come sundown. So I keep comin back to the same question. If it aint what you lost that is more than you can bear then maybe it's what you wont lose. What you'd rather die than to give up.

White   But if you die you will give it up.

Black   No you wont. You wont be here.

White   Well. I cant help you. Letting it all go is the place I finally got to. It took a lot of work to get there and if there is one thing I would be unwilling to give up it is exactly that.

Black   You got any other way of sayin that?

White   The one thing I wont give up is giving up. I expect that to carry me through. I'm depending on it. The things I believed in were very frail. As I said. They wont be around for long and neither will I. But I dont think that's really the reason for my decision. I think it goes deeper. You can acclimate yourself to loss. You have to. I mean, you like music, right?

Black   Yes I do.

White   Who's the greatest composer you know of?

Black   John Coltrane. Hands down.

White   Do you think his music will last forever?

Black   Well. Forever's a long time, Professor. So I got to say no. It wont.

White   But that doesnt make it worthless, does it?

Black   No it dont.

White   You give up the world line by line. Stoically. And then one day you realize that your courage is farcical. It doesnt mean anything. You've become an accomplice in your own annihilation and there is nothing you can do about it. Everything you do closes a door somewhere ahead of you. And finally there is only one door left.

Black   That's a dark world, Professor.

White   Yes.

Black   What's the worst thing ever happen to you?

White   Getting snatched off a subway platform one morning by an emissary of Jesus.

Black   I'm serious.

White   So am I.

Black   Before this mornin. What was the worst thing.

White   I dont know.

Black   Well, let's pretend you dont know then. Still, do you reckon it was about you? Or about somebody close to you?

White   Probably someone close to me.

Black   I think that's probably right. Dont that tell you somethin?

White   Yes. Dont get close to people.

Black   You a hard case, man.

White   How else could I win your love?

Black   You probably right. Let me try this. I dont believe that the world can be better than what you allow it to be. Dark a world as you live in, they aint goin to be a whole lot of surprises in the way of good news.

White   I'm sure that's true.

Black   Well jubilation. Listen at the professor.

White   But I'm at a loss as to how to bring myself to believe in some most excellent world when I already know that it doesnt exist.

Black   Most excellent.

White   Yes.

Black   I sure do like that. Most excellent.

White   Do you actually believe in such a world?

Black   Yes I do, Professor. Yes I do. I think it's there for the askin. You got to get in the right line. Buy the right ticket. Take that regular commuter train and stay off the express. Stay on the platform with your fellow commuter. You might even want to nod at him. Maybe even say hello. All of them is travelers too. And they's some of em been places that most people dont want to go to. They didnt neither. They might even tell you how they got there and maybe save you a trip you'll be thankful you didnt take.

White   Yes. Well, that's not going to happen.

Black   Why not?

White   Because I dont believe in that world. I just want to take the train. Look, why dont I just go?

Black   How about some more coffee?

White   No thank you.

Black   What can I do?

White   Maybe you just need to accept that you're in over your head.

Black   I do accept it. It dont let me off the hook though.

White   You think I dont understand. But I'm not sure you'd want to listen to the things I do understand.

Black   Try me.

White   It would just upset you.

Black   I been upset before.

White   It's worse than you think.

Black   That's all right.

White   You dont want to hear this.

Black   Yes I do. I got no choice.

The professor leans back and studies the black.

White   Okay. Maybe you're right. Well, here's my news, Reverend. I yearn for the darkness. I pray for death. Real death. If I thought that in death I would meet the people I've known in life I dont know what I'd do. That would be the ultimate horror. The ultimate despair. If I had to meet my mother again and start all of that all over, only this time without the prospect of death to look forward to? Well. That would be the final nightmare. Kafka on wheels.

Black   Damn, Professor. You dont want to see you own mama?

White   No. I dont. I told you this would upset you. I want the dead to be dead. Forever. And I want to be one of them. Except that of course you cant be one of them. You cant be one of the dead because what has no existence can have no community. No community. My heart warms just thinking about it. Silence. *Black-ness. Aloneness. Peace.* And all of it only a heartbeat away.

Black　Damn, Professor.

White　Let me finish. I dont regard my state of mind as some pessimistic view of the world. I regard it as the world itself. Evolution cannot avoid bringing intelligent life ultimately to an awareness of one thing above all else and that one thing is futility.

Black　Mm. If I'm understandin you right you sayin that everbody that aint just eat up with the dumb-ass ought to be suicidal.

White　Yes.

Black　You aint shittin me?

White　No. I'm not shitting you. If people saw the world for what it truly is. Saw their lives for what they truly are. Without dreams or illusions. I dont believe they could offer the first reason why they should not elect to die as soon as possible.

Black   Damn, Professor.

White   (Coldly) I dont believe in God. Can you understand that? Look around you man. Cant you see? The clamor and din of those in torment has to be the sound most pleasing to his ear. And I loathe these discussions. The argument of the village atheist whose single passion is to revile endlessly that which he denies the existence of in the first place. Your fellowship is a fellowship of pain and nothing more. And if that pain were actually collective instead of simply reiterative then the sheer weight of it would drag the world from the walls of the universe and send it crashing and burning through whatever night it might yet be capable of engendering until it was not even ash. And justice? Brotherhood? Eternal life? Good god, man. Show me a religion that prepares one for death. For nothingness. There's a church I might enter. Yours prepares one only for more life. For dreams and illusions and lies. If you could banish the fear of death from men's hearts they wouldnt live a day. Who would want this nightmare if not for fear of the next? The shadow of the axe hangs over every joy. Every road ends in death. Or worse. Every friendship. Every love. Torment, betrayal, loss, suffering, pain, age, indignity, and hideous lingering illness. All with a single conclusion. For you and for every one and every thing that you have chosen to care for. There's the true brotherhood. The true fellowship. And everyone is a member for life. You tell me that my brother is my salvation? My salvation? Well then damn him. Damn him in every shape and form and guise. Do I see myself in him? Yes. I do. And what I see sickens me. Do you understand me? *Can* you understand me?

The black sits with his head lowered.

White   I'm sorry.

Black   That's all right.

White   No. I'm sorry.

The black looks up at him.

Black   How long you felt like this?

White   All my life.

Black   And that's the truth.

White   It's worse than that.

Black   I dont see what could be worse than that.

White   Rage is really only for the good days. The truth is there's little of that left. The truth is that the forms I see have been slowly emptied out. They no longer have any content. They are shapes only. A train, a wall, a world. Or a man. A thing dangling in senseless articulation in a howling void. No meaning to its life. Its words. Why would I seek the company of such a thing? Why?

Black   Damn.

White   You see what it is you've saved.

Black   Tried to save. Am tryin. Tryin hard.

White   Yes.

Black   Who is my brother.

White   Your brother.

Black   Yes.

White   Is that why I'm here? In your apartment?

Black   No. But it's why I am.

White   You asked what I was a professor of. I'm a professor of darkness. The night in day's clothing. And now I wish you all the very best but I must go.

He pushes back his chair and rises.

Black   Just stay a few more minutes.

White   No. No more time. Goodbye.

He turns toward the door and the black rises.

Black   Come on, Professor. We can talk about somethin else. I promise.

White   I dont want to talk about something else.

Black   Dont go out there. You know what's out there.

White   Oh yes. Indeed I do. I know what is out there and I know who is out there. I rush to nuzzle his bony cheek. No doubt he'll be surprised to find himself so cherished. And as I cling to his

neck I will whisper in that dry and ancient ear:
Here I am. Here I am. Now open the door.

Black Dont do it, Professor.

White I'm sorry. You're a kind man, but I have to go.
I've heard you out and you've heard me and
there's no more to say. Your God must have
once stood in a dawn of infinite possibility and
this is what he's made of it. And now it is draw-
ing to a close. You say that I want God's love. I
dont. Perhaps I want forgiveness, but there is
no one to ask it of. And there is no going back.
No setting things right. Perhaps once. Not
now. Now there is only the hope of nothingness. I cling to that hope. Now open the door.
Please.

Black Dont do it.

White Open the door.

*The black undoes the chains. They rattle to the floor. He
opens the door and the professor exits. The black stands in
the doorway looking down the hall.*

Black Professor? I know you dont mean them words.
Professor? I'm goin to be there in the mornin.

I'll be there. You hear? I'll be there in the mornin.

He collapses to his knees in the doorway, all but weeping.

Black   I'll be there.

He looks up.

Black   He didnt mean them words. You know he didnt.
         You know he didnt. I dont understand what
         you sent me down there for. I dont understand
         it. If you wanted me to help him how come you
         didnt give me the words? You give em to him.
         What about me?

He kneels weeping rocking back and forth.

Black   That's all right. That's all right. If you never
         speak again you know I'll keep your word. You
         know I will. You know I'm good for it.

He lifts his head.

Black   Is that okay? Is that okay?

THE END

The World Premiere of *The Sunset Limited* was presented in
May 2006 by Steppenwolf Theatre Company of Chicago.
Martha Lavey, Artistic Director and David Hawkanson,
Executive Director. The New York Premiere was presented
by Steppenwolf Theatre Company at the 59E59 Theatre
in October 2006.

Both productions were directed by Sheldon Patinkin, with
scenic design by Scott Neale, costume design by Tatjana
Radisic, lighting design by Keith Parham, sound design
by Martha Wegener, casting by Erica Daniels, and
dramaturgy by Ed Sobel.

Cast
Black: Freeman Coffey
White: Austin Pendleton

All inquiries concerning performance rights to this work
should be addressed to the author's agent, International
Creative Management, Inc., Attn: Amanda Urban,
40 West 57th Street, New York, NY 10019.